KITCHEN

KAMA

SUTRA

KITCHEN KAMA SUTRA

50 Ways to Seduce Each Other Outside the Bedroom

ALEX WILLIAMS

THREE
RIVERS
PRESS

Text © 2006 Alex Williams
Design © 2006 by IVY PRESS Limited

ISBN 13: 987-0-307-33985-0

This book was conceived,
designed, and produced by:
IVY PRESS limited
The Old Candlemakers, West Street,
Lewes, East Sussex, BN 2NZ, UK.

Creative Director Peter Bridgewater
Publisher Jason Hook
Editorial Director Caroline Earle
Senior Project Editors Susie Behar/Emily Gibson
Art Director Sarah Howerd
Designer Joanna Clinch
Illustrations Sarah Young

Originated and printed in Thailand

Library of Congress Publication Data is available upon request.

10 9 8 7 6 5 4 3 2 1

First U.S. Edition

Disclaimer
The material in this book is for informational purposes only. The author and publisher
expressly disclaim responsibility for any injury or damage that may result from the use or
application of the information contained in this book. If you suffer from any health problems
or special conditions, you should use proper discretion, in consultation with a health care
practitioner, before undertaking the techniques described in this book.

~ CONTENTS ~

Mention the *Kama Sutra* to most people and the reaction you're most likely to get is a smirk. *Kama Sutra*? That's the kinky Indian sex-and-saris guide isn't it? The reality is very different. The *Kama Sutra* is an ancient text that has become more legend than legacy over the last 5,000 years, misinterpreted as a sexual gymnastics manual and dictionary of style over content.

The *Kama Sutra* was written with a higher intention than pure sexual titillation. It was originally an exploration of one of the "three necessities" of Hinduism: (1) *artha*, the material goods which assure survival; (2) *dharma*, the moral nature which maintains the cohesion and duration of the species; and (3) *kama*, love and the pleasures of the senses: hearing, feeling, seeing, tasting, and smelling, assisted by the mind and the soul. To get the best out of life, it said, we need to make sure that each of these boxes is ticked. Let's call them the bare necessities of life.

In *Kitchen Kama Sutra*, we've been inspired by the wise words of Vatsayana who compiled the "rules of love" in the 4th century A.D. It was Vatsayana who believed that a better understanding of sexuality would lead to a better society. *Sutra* is the poetry in which his words sang to generations of lovers; it's with a modern twist that we encourage this ancient wisdom to echo around your house.

In case you're not familiar with the words of the wise, we'll be referring to the penis as a *lingam* here, and the vagina as a *yoni*.

WHAT THE SYMBOLS MEAN

⁓ DIFFICULTY ⁓
♥ EASY LOVER
♡ YOU'LL GET THE HANG OF IT
♥ TAKES A BIT OF PRACTICE

⁓ TIME REQUIRED ⁓
⧖ GREAT FOR A QUICKIE
⧖ DO IT WHILE THE DINNER'S COOKING
⧗ NEEDS A SLOW HAND

⁓ FLEXIBILITY ⁓
🦵 NO CONTORTION REQUIRED
🦵 A LITTLE CONTORTION
🦵 FLEX YOUR MUSCLES

⁓ ADDITIONAL EQUIPMENT REQUIRED ⁓
🔨 NO EQUIPMENT REQUIRED
🔨 A FEW PROPS
🔨 GET YOUR TOOLBOX OUT

The central hallway is the first thing you see when you enter a home. It sets the tone for everything that follows. Walking through the front door and looking into the hallway is like taking the coat from your lover and looking at what lies underneath. Do you see gray walls, forbidding and cold? Do you see seductive red paint, with warm lighting and thick rugs? You set the tone, you dictate the game.

Don't rush straight into the house. Be still and breathe for a moment. Think of this stage as clearing the pathway in your mind for what is to follow. Focus on the seven chakras, from the rootsy sexual chakra in your anus through the emotional center of your belly where the heat of your desire is warming your very soul. Now breathe into your solar plexus in the middle of your chest. This is where your power lies. Breathe. What's the hurry? So he's waiting for you. Let him wait.

~ KNOCKING *on the* DOOR ~

J ust as you don't enter the house by breaking through a window, so you don't enter a woman by ripping her clothes off. You show respect and knock on the door. You ask permission. It's only polite. If the door opens, walk in. Take your time; don't rush. You are being invited in. Treat that invitation with respect.

Just as this is the beginning of your journey through the house, so it is the beginning of your sexual journey. It starts with a kiss. But don't imagine that a peck will do: the *Kama Sutra* has a name for that, "The Nominal" (*Nimittaka*). Vatsayana instead suggests "The Vibrant" (*Sphuritaka*) where he touches her mouth with just his upper lip, or "The Rubbing" (*Ghattitaka*), in which she covers his eyes and gently runs her tongue over his lips.

Why not follow Vatsayana's suggestion of a kissing game? You kiss each other—and the first to seize the other's lips is the winner. This you must do by surprise. A little tip: let the woman win. You won't regret it.

♡ YOU'LL GET THE HANG OF IT   ✗ DO IT WHILE THE DINNER'S COOKING
    NO CONTORTION REQUIRED   ♟ NO EQUIPMENT REQUIRED

COMING *Through*
~ *the* FRONT DOOR ~

Now just imagine . . . There's a knock on the front door. It's early; the lady of the house is not expecting anyone. She opens the door. She's wearing only a sheer silk robe. Her hair is wet. Maybe she's just come out of the shower.

There's a man at the door. He shows her his card. He says he's here to check her hot water, to see if the pressure is right. She stands aside, and he brushes past her. His cold outdoor clothes disturb her delicate silk. She asks if there's anything the man needs. "No, I'm fine," he replies. He takes his coat off and asks where her boiler is. She looks at him and asks him to follow her. She leans down and, as she opens the cupboard, her robe falls open.

The man reaches over to where the pressure control is and brushes her exposed breast. The woman gasps and, as she falls forward, she turns the control up. He plays it straight, telling her that he'll have to make a few readjustments to bring the temperature down. She reaches over to him and suggests that first they turn it up some more . . .

♥ EASY LOVER   ⚔ GREAT FOR A QUICKIE
↙ NO CONTORTION REQUIRED   ⚲ NO EQUIPMENT REQUIRED

～ *The* HAT STAND ～

Don't pass by your hat stand so quickly today. As a piece of furniture, it exists purely to help you take your clothes off. It holds them for you. It is your servant. Its physicality is, of course, phallic, and if Vatsayana had had that totem in his hallway, there would have been another chapter of the *Kama Sutra*.

When you next walk in together, take your partner's coat and hang it on the hat stand. Offer her yours. If she walks on, hold her back. Take her top off. Put it on the hat stand. Offer her yours. Carry on this process. Say nothing. The sexual tension comes from both the unexpected and the unknowing.

As you load more and more clothes on to the hat stand, it groans under the unexpected weight of its load. Tell your partner it's not the only moaning sound she will hear that night.

Before she has time to resist, attempt the *Sthita* ("Steadied"), a position designed for making love while standing and leaning against a wall. Scoop her into your hands, her arms around your neck. Her thighs grip your waist, while her feet push back against the wall behind you. She holds on to your neck, opening her yoni to you.

♥ EASY LOVER   ✖ GREAT FOR A QUICKIE
⚡ NO CONTORTION REQUIRED   ▼ NO EQUIPMENT REQUIRED

～ *The* STAIRS, *Going Up* ～

If the bedroom is the primary palace of pleasure, then the approach road—the stairs leading up—is the avenue of anticipation. Take your partner's hand and gently lead her to the stairs. Imply that the reason you're going upstairs is to go to the bedroom—but every time your partner tries to move up the stairs, stop her. Anticipation is key.

Allow minimal progress, maybe a few steps at a time. As your partner moves forward, pull her back. This will have the effect of making her crawl up the stairs, and this is where you want her.

As she is crawling, move in. You're behind her so she cannot see what you're about to do. Grab her ankles as she's crawling away from you and lift her legs up exposing her inner charms. Move on top of her and, as you enter her, let out a loud mewling "meow"—for this position is *Marjara* ("The Cat").

～

♡ YOU'LL GET THE HANG OF IT   ✗ GREAT FOR A QUICKIE
   A LITTLE CONTORTION   NO EQUIPMENT REQUIRED

⌒ *The* STAIRS, *Going Down* ⌒

To every yin there is a yang, and for every staircase going up, there is a staircase going down. But this one is different from the stairs that lead to the bedroom because this staircase leads down . . . down to the basement. Dark, empty, and unvisited, the basement is the place where anything is possible. A place to live out those fantasies, dark and silent. The perfect place to practice the art of scratching.

According to the *Kama Sutra*, scratching is as important a part of foreplay as the embrace, although it should be restricted to couples who find it mutually pleasurable. Stretching the boundaries, scratching can be just as much about pleasure as it is about pain.

Begin by pressing with your fingernails so softly that they don't leave a mark, and watch the hair on her body grow erect from your touch and the sound of your fingernails on her skin. If her body relaxes and she shows an increased willingness to unite her yoni with your lingam, press five nail marks in a half-moon on the back of her neck, navel, buttocks, or thighs. Make the imprint of the Peacock's Foot around her nipple by placing your thumb below, and your fingers above, and squeeze gently. Hear her moan in anticipation.

♡ YOU'LL GET THE HANG OF IT   ✗ DO IT WHILE THE DINNER'S COOKING
💪 FLEX YOUR MUSCLES   ⚡ NO EQUIPMENT REQUIRED

Push her forward—there's nowhere else to go. Caught in the dark, Vatsayana might suggest *Hirana*—"The Deer," perfect for men who are feeling horny. A rear-entry position, Vatsayana said of this: "The lady, eager for love, goes on all fours, humping her back like a doe, and you enjoy her from behind, rutting as though you'd lost all human nature." From this position you can scratch all you like.

THE CUPBOARD
⟿ UNDER *the* STAIRS ⟿

In many hallways there is a cupboard under the stairs. Small and cramped, there's no room to move in here. With two people in the cupboard every action is like *Twister*—put that arm here, that leg there. And it's all in the dark.

You can try out all your biting and scratching fantasies here. Nothing builds the sexual tension and expectation like gentle but forceful biting and scratching. It lights up the skin and awakens the raw emotion. If you love to express your passion by biting or scratching, press or bite hard enough to leave marks, but do not break the skin. Marks of passion on your skin excite admiration, Vatsayana says, and they remind you of past acts of love.

Start with The Hidden Bite, evident only by the redness of the skin; press down on your lover's skin with your whole mouth for The Swollen Bite. If he quivers for more, pause; then bite with two teeth only—The Point. And allow him to reply with more ritual biting—The Biting of the Boar, many broad rows of red teeth marks, impressed upon your breasts and shoulders.

♥ TAKES A BIT OF PRACTICE   ⏳ NEEDS A SLOW HAND
♣ FLEX YOUR MUSCLES   NO EQUIPMENT REQUIRED

Space is limited and you're pressed together. Sitting face to face, sit on his lap with your breasts pressed tight against his chest. Your heels are behind each other's waists. Now you both lean back clasping wrists, and rock slowly back and forth, feeling the walls of your confined space. Your partner will follow your movements gently, fearful because he cannot see anything. Close your eyes and he will do so too. Slowly he will let go his fear and give in to your body. Draw his lingam deeply into your body and squeeze repeatedly, allowing only tiny movements from your tangled bodies.

Back in the days of the *Kama Sutra*, the role of the courtesan, the ganika, was highly valued. She and her colleagues would keep their powerful male clients amused, with games and skills known as the 64 arts of sensual pleasure.

The ganika was an accomplished young woman, with talents in flower arranging, music, and dance, as well as interiors, clothes and body art, cookery, massage, and even magic. Tonight you are going to be the courtesan, offering a varied display of high-risk games to tease your lover with.

A ganika can be passive or active, but she's always in charge. Your man has paid you to service him tonight, so he'll follow your lead. His power is in your hands.

The set up is important. You'll have scattered rose petals over the living room floor and set up a chessboard. Run him a scented bath. Make sure the music is suitably refined. Or learn to play the piano. You'll be playing a duet in no time.

Don't forget to dress appropriately, perhaps in silk or a sari. And decorate your body with henna tattoos. Why not? You're not going anywhere tonight.

⌒ LET *the* DICE DECIDE ⌒

One of the most popular games of the ganika is "The Dice Game," a game of chance and high stakes. Your choice of dress should reflect the occasion; a robe or a sari, tightly bound, with nothing underneath. If it falls open, or the different positions allow a glimpse, inflaming your desire, remember the rules; let the dice decide what you do next.

Each player rolls the dice and the players must fulfill their obligation. The roll of the dice is non-negotiable. Forfeits can be imposed for refusing to play by the rules. Make your own dice with sexual suggestions on each of the six sides.

1. Lick Me
2. Be My Slave
3. Massage My Feet
4. Kiss Me
5. Take Me
6. Suck Me

♡ YOU'LL GET THE HANG OF IT   ⚱ GREAT FOR A QUICKIE
🔗 A LITTLE CONTORTION   🍸 A FEW PROPS

For a more traditional game, you could put different *Kama Sutra* positions on the dice. For example, choose six seated positions.

1. "The Tortoise": lie closely together in the "missionary" position, mouth to mouth, arms against arms, thighs against thighs.

2. "The Pair of Tongs": the man lies flat on his back, with the woman sitting astride him, knees bent. She draws his lingam deep inside, repeatedly squeezing it with the muscles of her yoni, and holding it tight.

3. "The Monkey": he sits, rotating his hips like a black bee within the cave of her thighs. (*See also* The Easy Chair, *pages 40–41.*)

4. "Crushing Spices": as above, but he faces away from her. (*See also* The Easy Chair.)

5. "Striking": she sits with raised thighs, her feet placed on either side of his waist. His lingam enters her yoni while (with permission) you rain gentle blows upon each other's bodies.

6. "The Foot Yoke": she sits with both knees drawn tight to her body and he mirrors this posture.

More advanced players should have two dice, one for the *Kama Sutra* positions within which they perform the commands of the more modern suggestions to the left.

F rom the days of the ancient scriptures to *The Thomas Crown Affair* with Steve McQueen and Faye Dunaway, chess has been understood as sex on a board. Whether it's the phallic shape of the pieces or the way players take and hold and move in order to get what they want, chess has captured the sexual imagination like few other games.

Consider, too, the final act of chess. Beaten and impotent, the King falls flat. Flaccid and powerless he lies there as the Queen moves her forces into position.

Place large candles on either side of the board. As the game progresses and the fall of the King becomes imminent, the candles get smaller and smaller. Their wax drips and falls, a symbol of what is to come. Practice breathing together; match your breaths in and out of your bodies. Inhale the perfume of your partner's skin.

With practice and timing you can control the flow of the game so that both his King and his resistance fall at the same time. The more adventurous can use the candle wax to discourage unwanted resistance.

At the close, he sits with his legs wide apart while you lower yourself down on top of him. When his lingam is fully overcome by your yoni, he presses your thighs together so that absolutely no further movement can take place.

Checkmate.

~ *The* GAMES WE PLAY ~

When we were children, games were fun and spontaneous. As adults they can be more challenging, even dangerous. Ganikas make no distinction—and tonight, you are the ganika who chooses the game.

Very often an apparently simple game can lead to the most unexpected of places. For instance, there is a children's memory game in which you construct a list of words and add to the list while remembering all that's gone before. Play this game with items of clothing. Whoever forgets something from the list must remove a piece of clothing. Add a forfeit and you'll soon find yourselves in all sorts of trouble.

Remember that this is sex play and so your list should be made up of things you'd like to do to each other—a kiss on the neck, a bite on the buttocks . . . And whatever you forget from the list, you must do. An idea for a forfeit? Sit her on your lap facing you. Lift her ankles and pull them behind your neck. This is a punishment. She must allow you to enter her while grabbing hold of her feet to help your thrusting motion. This position is *Padma* ("The Lotus"): "Sitting facing her, grasp her

♡ YOU'LL GET THE HANG OF IT   ✗ NEEDS A SLOW HAND
🦶 FLEX YOUR MUSCLES   👤 NO EQUIPMENT REQUIRED

ankles and fasten them like a chain behind your neck, and she grips her toes as you make love."

The *Kama Sutra* warns that this is a position that needs practice, skill, and flexibility, but the stimulation of the man's lingam and the woman's yoni is at its peak. Once you have mastered this position, you can make good use of your hands to explore her body, and as it's a forfeit, she can do nothing to resist.

⌐ KISSING *the* ROD ⌐

T he Oriental road to pleasure has always been about the stimulation of all five senses. Think about what stimulates your master's sight, his smell, his touch. You attend to what he can hear and what he can smell when you set up the chamber of pleasure. Now it's time for you to attend to what he can feel. This is the most intimate service you can offer and one that goes straight to the core of his sexual being.

Close the curtains to the world outside, light the candles on the mantelpiece and a fire in the hearth. Now, settle at his feet, and become a servant to his urgent needs at the end of a hard day.

In the *Kama Sutra*, the act of fellatio is known by the more delicate phrase "sucking a mango fruit." Begin by taking his lingam in your hand and repeatedly lick upward, first on one side and then the other. When you get to the top, gently flick the underside with your tongue. Kiss it as though you were kissing his lower lip.

"Fired by passion," wrote Vatsayana, "she takes the lingam deep into her mouth, pulling upon it and sucking as vigorously as though she were stripping clean a mango-stone. This is called *Amrachushita*."

♡ YOU'LL GET THE HANG OF IT   ⚔ NEEDS A SLOW HAND
⚙ NO CONTORTION REQUIRED   ♟ NO EQUIPMENT REQUIRED

The *Kama Sutra* also has some good advice for the act of swallowing— if you choose to. "When she senses that your orgasm is imminent, she swallows up the whole penis, sucking and working upon it with lips and tongue until you spend: this is *Sangara*."

~ *The* ART *of* ~
STORYTELLING

The ganika asks her master "How was your day today?" "The strangest thing happened," he answers. "I went to the stationery cupboard to get a new notebook. While I was there, Miss Jones from Accounting came in. Her pencil skirt skimmed her taut bottom and her breasts strained against her tight white blouse. Despite how tightly she'd tied it up, wisps of her dark hair escaped from her bun. She bent down to get a box of pens from one of the lower shelves and, as she bent down, I could see that she didn't have any panties on. She realized that I'd noticed, because her cheeks reddened in embarrassment. I couldn't help myself—we both knew she'd been waiting for us to be alone. I reached under her skirt and . . ."

A story is just a story. What counts is the way you tell it. As he seduces you with words, he pulls you in both spiritually and physically. Pay full attention and allow yourself to be aroused by fantasies.

Kaurma ("The Tortoise") is an intimate position where you sit facing each other, his lingam inside your yoni. You hold each other's hands and—maybe, if he's been practicing his yoga—he can caress

♥ TAKES A BIT OF PRACTICE   ✗ NEEDS A SLOW HAND
🔗 A LITTLE CONTORTION   ♟ NO EQUIPMENT REQUIRED

your breasts with his feet. He pulls you closer. Your head is spinning with his story. Is it real? Is there a Miss Jones in Accounting? His story is driving you wild with jealousy, but he calms you, putting his feet against your chest and gently playing with your nipples with his feet. He's teasing you. You pull him deeper inside you, just to make sure. Then you can begin your own story, taking him deeper into the fantasy world of the courtesan.

Since time began, music and dance have been used as instruments of seduction. In the old days, both courtesans and ladies of the court would be skilled in the musical arts. If you already play a musical instrument or write songs, you'll know what effect it has on your partner. And even if you can't play a note, you must know how to work the CD player.

Set the scene—the lighting, the cushions, the ambience. Perfume the air with incense. Cast your mind back to the days of the *Kama Sutra* and dress accordingly.

The Dance of the Seven Veils is stripping as art, stripping as tease. Tell him that he can look, but not touch. Touch yourself over your clothes; move slowly and seductively. When you remove your clothes, lower your eyes and act shy—Vatsayana says that even if a woman wants a man very much, she should resist his attempts. It is only when she is certain that he truly loves her that she should give herself to him.

As the last veil falls, your man will need your tenderest attention. Kneel in front of him, and spreading your knees wide, lean back to

♥ TAKES A BIT OF PRACTICE   ✗ DO IT WHILE THE DINNER'S COOKING
♪ FLEX YOUR MUSCLES   ♟ A FEW PROPS NEEDED

rest on your elbows. If you've been practicing your yoga, you will be able go all the way back, resting your head on the floor, and breathe into the stretch while he breathes into you.

He kisses and licks your inner thighs as you play with your breasts and nipples. Vatsayana would suggest *Jihva-bhramanaka* ("Circling Tongue"), a deliciously sensual cunnilingus. He suggests using all the senses. Your yoni is a beautiful flower—he closes his eyes; pausing to taste and feel you; taking in your scent.

"Now spread, indeed cleave asunder, that archway with your nose", he wrote, "and let your tongue gently probe her yoni, with your nose, lips and chin slowly circling." From within your yoni, he licks upwards, using light strokes on each side of your clitoris in turn. Using deep and shallow movements, he moves up and down as well as in and out.

Let him pleasure you—lie back, relax, and come in bliss.

The focal point in most living rooms is the television—the box. There are obvious ways in which that particular box can be used to add sexual spice to an evening—and who hasn't watched films for that purpose? But the *Kama Sutra* is about being inventive and why watch someone else when you can watch yourselves? Try hooking up your camcorder and setting it to record.

Vatsayana didn't have a TV but he did include a Box in his compilation. For those who need to "receive smaller sizes," "The Box" (*Samputaka*), in which lovers lie face to face, side by side, or one on top of the other, is the optimum position to get started. Call it the missionary position if you like, but if the woman squeezes her legs together after he enters her, "in the case of the hare (a man of smaller size) . . . the box position is guaranteed to allow him to find pleasure. If an elephant woman (a well-endowed woman) has a hare partner, she will be able to satisfy him in the box position."

And to show his evenhandedness, The Box, according to Vatsayana, is also the best position for two women.

♡ YOU'LL GET THE HANG OF IT   ⌛ DO IT WHILE THE DINNER'S COOKING
   ⚙ A LITTLE CONTORTION   ♦ NO EQUIPMENT REQUIRED

Vatsayana was no prude, and he understood that sometimes we like to be watched. Tonight, leave the curtains open—just a bit.

Lie your partner down on the floor, in front of the fish tank if you have one. Kiss all over his body with the "puckering" motion of a goldfish. This will tease him, as his skin is simultaneously being sucked and kissed—a delicious action.

Move from the nape of his neck down his spine. Keep the touch light. As you reach further down his back, maybe add a licking motion. Move toward his buttocks but just before you get there, move around to the sides and go back up again, increasing the heat and the touch.

Lying face to face on your sides, attempt "The Crow" (*Kakila*) by placing your head on his thigh, encouraging him to do the same. "In this position," wrote Vatsayana, "both seize each other's organ with their mouth. Like crows they peck at each other, drinking each other's secretions in the heat of their passion."

♡ YOU'LL GET THE HANG OF IT   ✗ DO IT WHILE THE DINNER'S COOKING
🐚 A LITTLE CONTORTION   ⌛ NO EQUIPMENT REQUIRED

⌒ *The* EASY CHAIR ⌒

Most of the situations described in the *Kama Sutra* concentrate on positions where you can move around. But the armchair is in many ways the perfect place to make love. You are held together by the shape of the chair. You sit upright, you cannot move sideways, you can't roll over. All thoughts of bedroom athleticism are abandoned as you lock together, held tight by the structure of the chair.

Sit on his lap, looking at each other, buzzing with expectation. Feel waves of energy flow between you. He dives into your honey pot with his lingam, and he lifts you up slightly, moving you backward and forward as you are impaled on his lingam. You can also sit on him, rotating your hips like "a black bee." This is *Markata* ("The Monkey").

Like the great tantrics, the action is on the inside. Tantrics believed that time was made for lovers but it took skill to make it your friend, particularly if your desire was likely to reach boiling point before your appetite had been truly whetted. The *Kama Sutra* suggested the "Mare's Trick" of gripping his lingam with your yoni's vice, squeezing and stroking it, holding it inside you for a

♡ YOU'LL GET THE HANG OF IT   ✗ DO IT WHILE THE DINNER'S COOKING
🐌 A LITTLE CONTORTION   🍸 A FEW PROPS

hundred heartbeats. The *Kama Sutra* calls this *Samdamsha* ("The Tongs"). He'll call it bliss. If you don't know how to hold him for a hundred heartbeats go to a pilates class. It will add a completely new dimension to your love life.

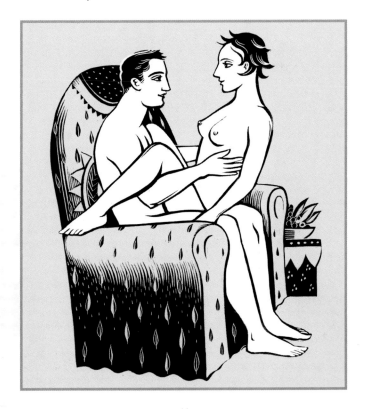

The most important sexual organ is the brain, so it's unsurprising that textures and layers so often figure into women's fantasies. Silk skirts and heavy petticoats under which furtive fingers find their pleasure, crisp Egyptian cotton sheets and soft velvet bedspreads— these are the fabrics of female fantasy. In the dining room, consider the tablecloth. Draped over the table, trailing luxuriously down to the carpet, it covers everything. Perhaps you bend down to retrieve a fallen glass and get distracted. After all, would anyone know if someone was underneath? What could you get away with? A tablecloth can be cleared just as soon as it's laid. Clear some space. So you spill a couple of glasses of wine. That's not all that you'll be spilling.

In the dining room, as in the kitchen, remember that sex is like food: the more mess you make, the more fun you have.

WHAT TO WEAR *to the*
◦◦ DINNER TABLE ◦◦

Choose your textures carefully—remember that for a woman, the feel of cool silk against a warm thigh is enough to get her cooking before you've even started the sauce.

The saris of the *Kama Sutra* days ensured that the woman would look demure, but allowed for delicious discovery. The shimmering delicacy of saris also allow for multi-layering . . . Every time you reach under one layer, what might you reach? Another layer or nirvana itself?

And for him? A loose satin robe or cotton trousers with nothing underneath perhaps. Or maybe the feel of a suit against her silk, both to arouse and deny her appetite.

"He passes his hand over the front of her body," wrote Vatsayana, "going as far as the top of the thigh, then caressing it. He calms her, smothering her with kisses, and sliding his hand between her thighs, strokes her secret parts." To make things more interesting at the dinner table, bring your feet into play. A caress with the feet can be even more sensual than the hand—certainly more

♥ EASY LOVER   ✗ DO IT WHILE THE DINNER'S COOKING
🗲 NO CONTORTION   ♟ NO EQUIPMENT REQUIRED

unusual. You won't be needing your shoes tonight. Perform a foot ritual on each other (*see* Get Off On the Right Foot, *pages 74–75*), and your toes will be itching for some action. Gently raise your foot to play with the edges of her silk robes, casually parting her calves and walking up to her inner thighs.

⌒ TASTE *That* ⌒

As all good cooks know, a key part of the pleasure of any meal is the way the food is presented. Careful place settings, fine china, and the arrangement of the food on the plates all add to the experience. Tonight is cause for an extra-special place setting.

Blindfold your partner. Take her clothes off slowly and lead her through to the dining room. Lie her down on the dining room table. The body in front of you is now your tablecloth—the base to eat your food from. No cutlery necessary.

According to the *Kama Sutra*, stirring the emotions provides a meaty prelude to sex. Spilling your starter onto her naked breasts, especially if it is something invigorating such as gazpacho or chilled melon, is sure to upset her and generate some passion.

After the starter you can move on to the main course. If this were the India of 5,000 years ago, you would have a delicious buffet of spiced delicacies. Try some crispy fried tiger shrimp with coriander, garlic, and ginger dipping sauce, bite-sized chicken tikka with mango chutney to smooth into any crevices, and some cold raita perhaps to cool her down.

❤ EASY LOVER   ⚔ NEEDS A SLOW HAND
🔧 NO CONTORTION REQUIRED   🍴 GET YOUR TOOLBOX OUT

For dessert, what about lingam-shaped kulfi, the ice cream so loved by Indians of today? Perhaps a little modern twist with warm, slippery chocolate sauce? Trickle it down her body to her yoni . . . It is, after all, where all juices begin and end.

Nine-and-a-Half
～ MINUTES ～

How selfish of you to help yourself while your partner just lies there. You're sated but she's naked and blindfolded. She's hungry, but what should you give her? Something hot? Something cold? Something dry? Maybe something wet.

"Keep a little mystery in your marriage," said Vatsayana. "Keep her guessing and she'll be yours forever." If you've exhausted all your ideas in the first flush of your romance, remember what she loved best when you were first courting and tell her what she looked like when you took her to the edge of desire, promising her a rerun of the best bit of your own love story.

Offer her fruits, strawberries and cream, dangling them over her mouth and allowing the cream to dance around her lips before it spills onto her breasts.

Chocolate? Ayurvedics have long since said that a little of what you desire is good for the health, and modern science has finally agreed, so melt some bitter dark chocolate and, while still warm, paint it on her neck and lick delicately until she closes her eyes. Now

❤ EASY LOVER   ✖ NEEDS A SLOW HAND
🌿 NO CONTORTION REQUIRED   ⚲ A FEW PROPS

pour her a drink. Vodka? Ice and a slice? Don't waste it. Drip the ice delicately over her body, watch her wriggle and shiver as the icy sensation awakens her skin. Start by putting an ice cube in her mouth with a splash of the vodka, tonic, and lemon. Let it spill. You can lick it up later. Rub another cube over her body, across her breasts, down past her navel, over her clitoris, down and inside her, and, as we're looking for nerve endings, up into her anus. Expect a look of surprise that would make even Vatsayana smile.

∽ SAVOR *the* FLAVOR ∽

Now for a game for both of you to play. Eating with your hands is still the way to make the most of a delicious meal in India—the contact with the food on your fingers, the juices staining your palms. It's a sensual pleasure that reminds you of the flesh that you're putting in your mouth, playing with your tongue, nibbling with your teeth.

Forget your manners. Forget the plates, the cutlery, and the serving dishes. A rare steak, pink juices oozing out, is all you need tonight. Or perhaps a Japanese banquet of sashimi suggestively sliced on a board. Sink your fingers in and offer your lover the first bite, allowing him to take your fingers into his mouth to suck off every last bit. You can feel the flesh in his mouth, his tongue savoring the flavor, his teeth gently nibbling your fingers by mistake.

Can't get close enough to feed him properly? Move up onto the table; remember there are no plates or wine glasses to break. Kneeling in front of him, your silks part, offering a brief glimpse of the next course. As you offer him the next bite, instead you drop it in your lap . . .

♥ EASY LOVER   ⌛ NEEDS A SLOW HAND
    NO CONTORTION REQUIRED   ♀ A FEW PROPS

The courts of the Indian nobility were filled with courtesans and courtiers; plenty of people to invite to the lengthy feasts that filled the balmy nights. But to imagine that they did nothing except eat is quite wrong; who wants to feel stuffed with food when there's so much more on the menu?

But a dinner party in suburbia in December is a very different scenario to an Indian summer's feast 5,000 years ago, and to recreate the air of pure decadence, you're going to have to give the atmosphere some thought.

Choose your guests carefully; remember the bank managers are just as likely as the literary types to have the imagination to engage in your evening of erotic celebration. Now lay the clues. Handcuffs in the hall, silk sashes in the bathroom, ropes on the bed in the guest room where they'll leave their coats. Display a few well-chosen books to make sure that the temperature is raised before you've even served the chili. Plan your menu carefully, with aphrodisiacs such as oysters, asparagus, and figs with honey. By the time they're sipping their cocktails, they'll be expecting a very different kind of evening.

♥ EASY LOVER   ✗ NEEDS A SLOW HAND

   🔧 NO CONTORTION REQUIRED   🔧 GET YOUR TOOLBOX OUT

DIVINE OFFICE

The office is a place of serious endeavor. You go there to work. It's a place where order is the name of the game and where discipline is required. When you go into the office, it is for a purpose.

Everything in the office reflects this idea. There are cold surfaces, sharp edges. The furniture is functional rather than comfortable.

On the desk the objects are similarly severe: staplers, pens, rulers, paperweights, a computer, a printer, a phone. Things that are there for a reason. An office is not a frivolous place—and it isn't a place for frivolous thoughts.

But look again. What better place for a bit of role play? That whole "master and servant" thing works perfectly in the office. "Take a letter Miss Jones." The ruler that looked so lacking in promise a minute ago? Perfect punishment for Miss Jones. And what if a pair of panties were to get caught in the shredder?

The COMBAT *of the*
⌘ TONGUES ⌘

Y ou're in your office at home. It's an ordinary day where you're doing ordinary things in an ordinary way. Nothing wrong with that—we all have them. You're sitting at your desk contemplating life when, breaking the silence, you hear the dog bark. It's the mailman.

You don't pay much attention. What's there going to be apart from the usual collection of junk offers and predatory bills?

There's a knock on the office door. Hmm. That's odd.

"Er, yes?" you say.

The door opens and in walks your partner. She's wearing a buttoned-up skirt/jacket suit and a white blouse. Her hair is up in a bun. She seems to be waiting for your instruction. She licks her lips, and her eyes tell you what she is thinking.

You say nothing. You look up at her and motion to something on your desk. She looks down. You take her head and pull her lips toward yours. Vatsayana knew about power play and suggested a game called "Combat of the Tongues," a rough kiss which involves a thorough and vigorous exploration of each other's mouths.

♥ EASY LOVER   ✗ DO IT WHILE THE DINNER'S COOKING
✄ NO CONTORTION REQUIRED   ⚲ NO EQUIPMENT REQUIRED

You win; you're the boss and you dictate the play. The "Pressed Position," in which she is submissive to you, is the rule today. She lies on her back with her knees bent against her chest. You kneel in front of her, supporting her buttocks with your thighs as she presses her feet against your chest. Her yoni will be shortened and open in this position, so begin to thrust slowly and gently. Remember to tidy up the office afterward before getting on with your day.

~ *And cue . . .* ACTION! ~

Sometimes when you're hard at work, it all goes well. And sometimes it just doesn't flow at all. If it's not going the way it should, don't beat yourself up. Take some time out. Take your head on a trip away. Reach over to your shelves and find a DVD. A little outside stimulation won't do you any harm. You see a title, *Secretary*, starring James Spader and Maggie Gyllenhaal. As you watch the film, you start to get aroused. You call downstairs to your wife.

"Honey, could you just take a letter for me. There's something I need to do."

She looks at you, puzzled, but does as you ask. She sits down at the computer and begins to type. You get up and walk around to where she is. You stand behind her and, silently, undo your trousers, take out your lingam and begin to pleasure yourself.

She is distracted and makes a mistake. It's not good enough, you tell her. You order her to stand up, and you lift her skirt exposing her round buttocks. With one hand you take care of yourself, with the other, and with her permission, you smack her naked flesh. The *Kama Sutra* suggests various ritual blows that provoke arousal. If you

---

♥ EASY LOVER ⚔ GREAT FOR A QUICKIE
⚙ NO CONTORTION REQUIRED ♟ A FEW PROPS REQUIRED

are both game, try the four kinds of blows: the back of the hand, the fingertips and front of the open hand, the fist, and the palm of the hand. The shoulders, the head, the space between the breasts, the back, and the midriff are recommended.

With a final flourish, you ejaculate over her back.

"Thank you, that will be all," you say and return to your desk.

Now it's your turn. "Take off your shirt," you say. "I wonder if you'll like it so much when you're the victim." Vatsayana has nothing to offer in your oppressor's defense; he even recommends the punishment, "The Half Moon" (*Ardhachandra*) to leave your mark. "The semicircular mark left by the nail on the neck or below the breasts is called the half moon. Very cruel when done with the little finger, it is more permanent when done with the middle one."

He might protest, but you've got business to finish. Sit on the desk in front of him, and let him cup and lift your buttocks. He must start with your breasts and kiss you all the way down. If he's half the man we think he is, his tongue-tip will soon be probing your navel, before slithering down to your thighs and the outer lips of your yoni, and begin "to rotate skilfully in the archway of the love-god's dwelling and lap your love-water." This is what the Kama Sutra calls *Uchchushita* ("Sucked Up").

Feel the energy flow between you. Breathe deeply. He must worship you as a ferocious goddess, the fount of all life and the most sacred pleasure of living. Now, "stirring the root of her thighs, which

♥ EASY LOVER ⚔ NEEDS A SLOW HAND
🖋 NO CONTORTION REQUIRED ⛏ NO EQUIPMENT REQUIRED

her own hands are gripping and holding widely apart, your fluted tongue drinks at her sacred spring" in Vatsayana's version of a coffee break, *Kshobhaka* ("Stirring"). Heaven.

⟐ *Pick*, LICK, SEAL ⟐

Working together can be a joy if you know how to cooperate. Share out the tasks—many hands make light work. "Tell you what, I'll fold the letters, you put them in the envelopes. Don't you think it's hot in here? Let's take our clothes off."

"OK," she says. "We'll be done soon, and then . . ."

She looks at you with moist lips and suddenly you can see a much better use for them. She's kneeling there picking up envelopes, licking them and sealing them. Pick, lick, seal. Pick, lick, seal. Walk around so you're standing behind her. You grab your tie from the pile of clothes on the floor, and—very quietly—you blindfold her. She carries on with her task. Pick, lick, seal.

She's a professional, and she says nothing. You're the boss and she must do anything you ask of her. But you're not likely to abuse your position, are you? Instead, you might simply show her just what made you so good at what you do. You remember the words of the *Kama Sutra* on how to perform the perfect kiss: "With delicate fingertips, pinch the arched lips of her house of love very, very, slowly together, and kiss them as though you kissed her lower lip," said

♥ EASY LOVER   ✗ NEEDS A SLOW HAND
⚷ NO CONTORTION REQUIRED   ⚑ A FEW PROPS

Vatsayana of *Adhara-sphuritam* ("The Quivering Kiss"). "Let your tongue rest for a moment in the archway to the flower-bowed Lord's temple [the yoni] before entering to worship vigorously, causing her seed to flow: this is *Jihva-mardita*" ("The Tongue Massage"). Who says you can't take a break in the working day?

Intimacy is the best part of a relationship, the bit when all the chasing has been done and bedtime is as much about taking turns in the bathroom as it is about slipping into each other under the comforter. Remember that the bathroom can be just as much a playroom as the bedroom, with a little imagination. But before you get out the coconut oil, start with something closer to home.

As the only room in the house with a lock on it, the bathroom is made for intimacy. No one knows what goes on in the bathroom. No one asks; it's rude.

But before you get down to it, remember that intimacy is about respect. Check the door. Just as an undone button can signal intent, so too can an unlocked door.

The bathroom. There's no better place to get dirty than a place designed to get you clean.

⌁ A *Gentle* OPENER ⌁

Y ou think your partner loves you? Try this and you'll see what love is. It's a cold and wet outside, a real dog of a day. The traffic's always a nightmare on days like this. You know he's going to come home stressed to the gills.

Go upstairs into the bathroom. Run a nice, hot bath and, while the water's running, tip a few drops of ylang ylang into the water. Place candles around the tub and enjoy the aroma of the oils filling the air. Go downstairs and pick a few petals from that bouquet of flowers you've got in the living room and sprinkle them on to the surface. (Timing is all here—the bath must still be hot when he gets home.)

Meanwhile, the ylang ylang's aphrodisiac properties are beginning to have their effect. You check your watch. Ten minutes until the key turns in the lock. You settle into the bathroom chair and consider the use of that baby oil. Mmm, you've had a hard day too. You deserve a little rub.

Say nothing when he gets home. Take his coat and release a small inward smile. You know he always goes to the bathroom as soon as he comes in. Wait a few minutes until he's had a chance to

♥ EASY LOVER   ⌛ NEEDS A SLOW HAND
✎ NO CONTORTION REQUIRED   🍸 A FEW PROPS

66

relax into the water and then . . . quietly go and join him by the tub. Gently massage the water into his skin.

From here, it's only a step for you to join him in the water.

∽ WET, *Wet*, *Wet* ∽

ait until the bathroom door is open. This signals that she's happy to share her space. Give her a few minutes to settle herself and maybe wait until she's brushing her teeth, then come in quietly. Stand behind her. Cover her eyes with a silk scarf.

Gently take the toothbrush from her and continue the task. Move around and offer her some water in your cupped hands to rinse, then slowly use your fingers to massage her lips, inserting your forefinger occasionally into her mouth as if to check that the job has been done well. Swap your finger for your tongue, but only irregularly to keep her guessing. If she tries to kiss you, retreat. Only when she submits do you start again.

Vatsayana writes about many types of kiss in the *Kama Sutra*, but the bathroom is the place for *Ghattitaka*, "The Rubbing Kiss." "Holding her loosely, he covers her eyes with his hands. He then rubs his lover's lips with his tongue. He offers his lower lip into her open mouth which she seizes and sucks occasionally, and licks gently with her tongue." If you are both in a hurry—the morning commute to work can wait; she certainly can't—lift her robe and,

♥ EASY LOVER 　　✗ DO IT WHILE THE DINNER'S COOKING
🦶 NO CONTORTION REQUIRED 　　♟ A FEW PROPS

68

as she's still brushing, slip inside her from behind. Her brushing rhythm mirrors your thrusting rhythm. Carry on like this and she'll never need any more fillings.

⌒ MUD, GLORIOUS MUD ⌒

The bathroom is where you keep all your lotions and potions. Essential oils aren't called essential for nothing. If the skin needs softening up, this is the place.

But the *Kama Sutra* suggests that a committed lover will have more than a few bottles of ylang ylang in his bathroom cabinet. The bathroom is a place of indulgence, of sinking into sensual bliss where time is yours, and where there are no rules or boundaries in the pursuit of pleasure.

During the day go shopping and buy not just one mud face pack, but maybe twenty. When your partner gets home, take her into the bathroom, remove her clothes and wash her down. Wrap her in warm towels and make her feel like she's a queen.

Empty all the mud face packs into a large bowl and whip the mixture up. It's not just wrapping her in the mud that's the thrill, it's how you do it. Don't rush. Think about it. Make sure you apply the mixture thoroughly.

When you've finished, stand back and admire your work. If you have done this properly there will be two holes for her nipples to

♡ YOU'LL GET THE HANG OF IT ✕ NEEDS A SLOW HAND
🐾 NO CONTORTION REQUIRED ♟ A FEW PROPS

poke through and another gap between her thighs. Gently caress her clitoris while the mud dries. As much as she'd like to wriggle, she can't, for if she does, the mud will crack. Completely immobile, watch as she stiffens and submits to your touch.

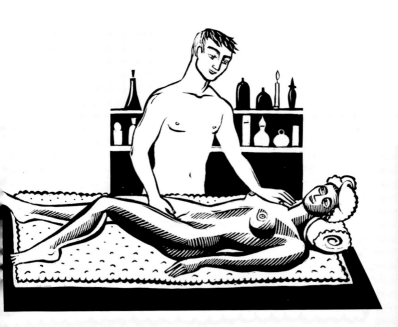

⁓ WHERE'S *the* SOAP... ⁓

According to the *Kama Sutra*, making love in the water is almost impossible, either immersed or half-immersed. Vatsayana said that respectable people wouldn't do such a thing, and while we respect the great man we must allow ourselves the luxury of dissent here. Making love to your partner in the bath is one of the great joys of life—even if it takes a little practice. So? You're not going anywhere are you?

Run your partner a bath, not forgetting to add those sensuous oils. Let him soak and relax in the water. Wash him, caress him, rub him. As he relaxes in the water, give him a facial, using a muslin cloth soaked in hot water to warm his tired brow. Massage in your favourite cleaners, taking care to rub his temples until he purrs. Inhale the perfumes wafting over the warm water. Then join him. If he had any resistance, he certainly won't now.

Your bodies flow together. The slightly oily nature of the water acts as a natural lubricant as you slide up and down each other. The waves increase as you slide, and the water splashes up and over the edges of the bath. Water gives a whole new dynamic. Things that

♥ TAKES A BIT OF PRACTICE   ✗ NEEDS A SLOW HAND
   A LITTLE CONTORTION   ♟ A FEW PROPS

seem normal on dry land are completely different here. Dive under, hold your nose, and try taking your partner in your mouth. Lick and taste how clean he is. Finally, lift your legs on to the sides of the bath. The only resistance you'll feel is the water against you as he thrusts.

GET OFF *on the*
⌁ RIGHT FOOT ⌁

I t's entirely logical that your feet are going to be sensitive: they are your point of contact with the soil, with the earth. They hold you, support you. Without your feet, where would you be? On your knees is where.

People talk about how feet are an important erogenous zone, how they are sensitive and how just one touch—the right touch—is enough to get the juices spinning. They knew about feet in the old days: reflexology is the modern expression of the ancient wisdom that says the feet are the root of all bodily truth.

Your lover has come home. He looks tired; his brow is furrowed and his back is aching. He goes to flop into the sofa and picks up the remote, but you have a better idea. Take him to the bathroom. (You've already made sure that the lighting and the atmosphere are in place.) Sit him down on the side of the bath, kiss him lightly on the lips and then . . . blindfold him. The senses work so much better when stimulated by the imagination—and nothing stimulates the mind so much as sensory deprivation.

❤ TAKES A BIT OF PRACTICE   ✗ NEEDS A SLOW HAND
   🔥 NO CONTORTION REQUIRED   ⚲ A FEW PROPS

Hold his feet. Rub them. Caress them. Manipulate them. Lick them.
Suck them. Get his big toe and rub it lengthways—it's amazing
how it looks like a little penis. And it's amazing how it can do what
a little penis can do.

This is your chance to out-Pollock Jackson himself. The bathroom is full of lotions and strange creams of every kind. Prepare a surface, turn up the heating, and lay out all the jars and bottles. All you need now is a canvas. By now you don't need to be told.

Let your partner lie on the bathroom floor, naked and ready, with plenty of warm towels beneath her. Warm the bottle in your hands and then dribble! Pink peppermint foot lotion. Light green aloe vera cream. What's that blue bottle over there? Shampoo? Never mind. The look is the creation.

Now it's time to massage with musk, saffron, and aloes mixed with cream. Body to body is how the Thai people do it—a sensual, slippery, and intimate move. But even Jackson Pollock used a brush at times, and now you can use yours. Try the toothbrush, that new electric one. Gently rub its vibrating head over her body and create beautiful patterns. Move the toothbrush head down between her legs and the shampoo won't be the only thing frothing up.

♥ EASY LOVER   ✖ NEEDS A SLOW HAND
⚐ NO CONTORTION REQUIRED   ♟ GET YOUR TOOLBOX OUT

The *Kama Sutra* recommends all kinds of standing positions for times when you can't wait to lie down. Vatsayana says, "Leaning on each other, she folds her legs, supported by the man's hands. Lifting first one of her feet then the other, the woman puts them in the man's hands, her sex open, facing him."

Standing up in the shower having sex with your partner is a classic position, and one that Vatsayana would have embraced—had they had power showers in the old days. As it is, you can adapt *Sthitarata* ("Standing Intercourse") to the shower. This position is best suited to a couple who are of similar height. You should stand with your legs apart for balance, and your knees bent to protect your back, so that your lingam can reach her yoni. She should spread her thighs, wrapping one of her legs around yours for deeper penetration. You will be able to control the depth of your thrusts by holding her thigh.

But consider this. She's got her legs wrapped around you, and it's slippery and wet and warm and slightly oily. She's drifting into that pre-orgasmic space, when you reach up to the shower head, switch it to power jet and place it about an inch from her clitoris.

♡ YOU'LL GET THE HANG OF IT   ⊠ DO IT WHILE THE DINNER'S COOKING
🎵 FLEX YOUR MUSCLES   ⌇ NO EQUIPMENT REQUIRED

∼ AND *at the* END... ∼

There's something very appealing about bad guys. You know you should disapprove but you like stepping beyond boundaries.

At the end of your bath lift your partner up and have her lean over the side of the tub. Arrange the shower head so that the water is falling onto her shoulders and rolling down her back. Be gentle. Have a large bottle of water-based massage lotion to hand—it's exactly the right consistency for what you have got in mind. The circumstances are right: she's hot, relaxed, and just about as ready as anyone's ever going to be.

Stand behind her and hold her tight. Massage her first, second, third chakras, moving your hands from her buttocks (chakra 1) onto her belly (chakra 2) and up to her breasts (chakra 3). Just as she starts to feel that tell-tale tingle... insert a well lubricated finger into her root chakra. According to the ancient scriptures, it's like earthing your power source. More lotion. Move it around. It's a curious thing, but you'd be surprised how much more malleable the human body is when it's this slippery.

♥ EASY LOVER   ⌛ NEEDS A SLOW HAND
⚔ NO CONTORTION REQUIRED   ▼ A FEW PROPS

The engine room of the house, the kitchen is the only place where you'll find both fire and ice, where you roast and where you freeze, where you prepare and where you feed.

The kitchen is a dangerous place, where knives cut and graters shred, where the heat of the oven is only matched by the fire of the emotions. You can use that heat to stoke the fires of your passion. Watch her. Wait till she's in the kitchen, preparing the food. As she slices and dices, come up behind her. Put your arms around her waist, just under her breasts. Run your fingernails lightly over her flesh. If she coos in anticipation, try the *Dash Rekha*, a small series of straight lines, through to "The Tiger's Claw" or *Vyaghranakha* where a line is drawn up toward the breasts, to "The Peacock's Claw" or *Mayurapadaka* where the nipples are seized by all five fingernails.

According to the *Kama Sutra*, "in the heat of the union, people are not aware of the parts of the body that they can scratch and those they should avoid," but—as Vatsayana might have said—if you can't stand the heat, get out of the kitchen.

⌣ SAUCY *Boy* ⌣

The kitchen is a place where you cook, where you take some raw ingredients and, through your manipulations, you turn them into a dish fit to eat.

"What would you like for dinner tonight, darling?" "I've bought a nice steak but it needs a bit of preparation."

As with all things, make your first move quietly and gently and take it from there. Wait until she's preparing a dish. Come up behind her and, slowly, lift her skirt. Lightly run your fingers over her as you reach for the kitchen scissors, and cut down the sides of her panties, using the tip to gently graze her thigh. Bite the back of her neck, marking her as she kneads the food, mirroring her actions, nibbling and caressing her as she molds the food to her wish.

Feed her. Push the food gently into her mouth and feel her teeth graze your fingers. Give her a taste of each flavor the tongue can distinguish: sour, sweet, salty, and bitter. Those plump, ripe figs wrapped in salty prosciutto were supposed to be starters, but who would notice if a couple went missing? Pass the parcels between you with your lips; stimulate each other with different textures.

♡ YOU'LL GET THE HANG OF IT   ⚓ DO IT WHILE THE DINNER'S COOKING   ∂ A LITTLE CONTORTION   ⚲ NO EQUIPMENT REQUIRED

Spread her legs as she tenderizes the meat. It's up to you to provide the stuffing. As she delicately oils the steaks, slide yourself inside her. She closes her eyes and continues to rub her meat as you push yourself deeper and deeper . . .

Just as you are about to come, you pull out and finish yourself off over her back. You saucy boy.

SLICE, DICE,
~ *Cut*, SCRATCH ~

There's so much cutting and chopping and slicing and dicing in the kitchen. It's all very aggressive. Some of that aggression is bound to influence how you feel and how you act.

Consider this. He's preparing a meal—cutting and slicing, chopping and stirring. Stand behind him and mirror his actions. Breathe deeply, down into your lungs, and take in his scent. Exhale strongly, so your diaphragm massages your heart. Share each other's *prana*, or vital energy. Slice, scratch. Cut, scratch. Chop, scratch. Dice, scratch, stir. The animal in him becomes the animal in you. Pretty soon the meal becomes lost in the passions you've unleashed.

"For any practice or aggression, the same practice or aggression should be inflicted by way of example. With blows and kisses, the same coin should be repaid." Try the *Dash Rekha*, a short straight line traced with the nails on any part of the body. Or what about "The Tiger Claw" (*Vyāghranakha*), a line curving inward, traced near the breast or on the face.

♡ YOU'LL GET THE HANG OF IT   ⌛ DO IT WHILE THE DINNER'S COOKING
🦶 A LITTLE CONTORTION   🍸 NO EQUIPMENT REQUIRED

Wherever we've been in the house we've used the ingredients found in that room as stimulants—and the kitchen is no different. Look around and it's all there. Olive oil creates a nice feel and is, as we all know, extremely healthy. Mayonnaise? Soy sauce? Guacamole? Careful of the chilis. The possibilities are endless.

It's hot enough to fry an egg in here and she's wearing a backless top. Pick up an egg and break it over her back. Watch the white and the yolk separate as the contents drip down her body . . .

Undress your partner and lie her down on the kitchen table. Pour the requisite amounts of flour, water, and yeast on the pit of her stomach. Mix them all together. Knead the dough like you need her. Push it and roll it and mix it and squeeze it. Press the dough down between her breasts.

You're way past the idea that this will become a loaf by now; this is more playdough. But remember the *Kama Sutra* is big on the arts, and haven't you always wanted to be a sculptor?

If your dough is really firm, roll it into a lingam shape, push it deep into her, thrusting in and out until she rises. Ancient India

♥ EASY LOVER   ✗ DO IT WHILE THE DINNER'S COOKING
   ⚬ A LITTLE CONTORTION   ♟ NO EQUIPMENT REQUIRED

may not have had batteries, but they would certainly have found a use for such a phallus. Watch as she rides it as if it were you, just as Vatsayana would have suggested. "If she now swings her hips in wide circles and makes figures of eight, as though she were riding on a seesaw," it is *Prenkholita* "The Swing." Careful; Vatsayana suggests that "This kind of intercourse is practiced with a virile female partner," and chances are that she is going to find herself making bread a little more often from now on.

89

A Traditional
STUFFING

You've invited some friends around for Sunday dinner. You're traditional types and you decide to do a full roast, complete with all the trimmings and stuffing.

It's an earthy dish, and part of the fun of it is in sourcing the ingredients. As you take them out of the fridge now, you remind each other of how they came to be there. As she dips the rosemary in olive oil to sprinkle lightly on the chicken, you take her back to the garden where you picked it early this morning and what she was wearing when she leaned down to pick it. She hadn't seen you behind her, but as she felt your hand between her bare legs, she buckled and fell to the ground as you knelt down behind her.

She laughs, but you can see her nipples grow erect. You remind her of the trip to the butcher in a summer dress and sandals, but little else. She had promised that she would buy her meat with nothing but a bit of cotton between her and the butcher. Again she laughs at the memory, but she is closer now. As you put the chicken in the oven, you notice that it's an hour until the guests arrive. Perfect.

EASY LOVER — DO IT WHILE THE DINNER'S COOKING
A LITTLE CONTORTION — NO EQUIPMENT REQUIRED

In The REALM *of the*
⌇ SENSES ⌇

There's nothing like re-creating a film for a bit of authentic role play. You could do the refrigerator scene from *Nine and a Half Weeks*, feeding each other blindfolded with strange and exotic fruits.

Only one person is blindfolded. This is about master and servant, lord and concubine, dominatrix and victim, and not about taking turns. Feed your passive partner a selection of foodstuffs: cherry tomatoes, chunks of cucumber, slices of avocado, dried apricots, wild honey, whatever you want. Before you put it in her mouth, ask her to guess what it might be, allowing her to smell it, maybe a tiny lick, a rub against a nipple to guess the texture.

If she doesn't guess, you are allowed to use the ingredients for your own pleasure. She won't resist. Vatsayana might have suggested "The Bird's Amusement" (*Chatakavilasa*) at a time like this: "Alternatively penetrating and half penetrating with the penis, striking 2, 3, 4 small blows inside the vagina, like the pecking of a bird." Then stop. Pause and give her another taste, to see if she gets it right this time. Prepare a suitable reward or punishment for her guesses.

♡ YOU'LL GET THE HANG OF IT   ✗ DO IT WHILE THE DINNER'S COOKING
   ⚙ A LITTLE CONTORTION   ⚲ NO EQUIPMENT REQUIRED

WE ALL SCREAM
⟶ *for* ICE CREAM ⟵

We all know the phrase "If you can't stand the heat get out of the kitchen" but the kitchen is also the place in the house where you'll find the most extreme cold. Ah yes, the freezer.

Take your lover into the kitchen. Greet your old friend, the blindfold, and place it over her eyes. Take off her clothes, take her hand, and lead her over to the kitchen table. Lie her down on it.

That big pot of ice cream you bought earlier now comes into its own. Rub it into her skin; it tingles and stimulates in the same way that an ice cube does, but while deliciously cold, it's also creamy and soft. Rub it all over her and her whole body will become sensitized.

Maybe now up the ante with some sorbet. Halfway between cream and ice, it's colder and sharper, but still malleable. Smooth it into her skin and into her body. Slide it in where it will fit. Into her mouth, into her vagina and—and this one will create a shiver—into her anus. There's only one problem: you got the ice cream in there, so you've got to get it out. Remember to choose a flavor you like.

♡ EASY LOVER   ✗ DO IT WHILE THE DINNER'S COOKING
   A LITTLE CONTORTION   ☿ NO EQUIPMENT REQUIRED

⌒ IMPLEMENT *Your* IDEAS ⌒

The kitchen is full of useful gadgets. Some of these can come in useful for purposes other than those they were designed for. Run the rolling pin up and down the length of her bare body. The soft bristles of a pastry brush can be used on naked skin to delicious effect. The cold metal of the egg whisk will give a gentle beating to a recalcitrant lover. And icing bags can be used for more than just decorating cakes. Tell her your thoughts and listen to her moan.

Pulling her onto the kitchen table, let her rest on her back as you pull her legs open and consider your next pleasure. Keep your chosen gadgets handy. Watch as her legs dangle helplessly from the edge of the table, her hair splayed out. Admire her as you stand between her legs, playing with yourself. Holding her gaze, telling her exactly what you are going to do, enter her. After four or five long, slow thrusts, hold still so her yoni can feel your lingam throb. Gently massage her clitoris—underneath and to each side. Thrust again. Pause. Repeat the process. Take your time. The art of cooking is all about patience.

♥ TAKES A BIT OF PRACTICE   ⌛ DO IT WHILE THE DINNER'S COOKING
   ⚭ A LITTLE CONTORTION   ♟ NO EQUIPMENT REQUIRED

You Really Must
⟿ COME AGAIN ⟿

There's nothing like cooking to raise the temperature, and kitchens are notorious as places where emotions run high. Invite your friends around and, just before they are due to arrive, take your partner on the table, by the stove, against the refrigerator. But don't bring him to climax. Each time you're near . . . stop and start again. "Catching your penis, the lady with dark eyes like upturned lotus petals guides it into her yoni, clings to you and shakes her buttocks": this is *Charunarikshita* ("Lovely Lady in Control").

Your partner will be feel thwarted and will come back for more. Make him beg. He is desperate. Act your passions out. Gently at first, and if you both enjoy it, the *Kama Sutra* recommends blows on the shoulders, the head, between the breasts, the back, the sexual area, and the sides; hitting with the side of the hand, with the palm, with the fist, and with the end of the fingers joined. Rage, but, however passionate you are, remain in control. Hold him inside of you and watch him carefully. Focus; take him to the brink. Do not let him come.

❤ EASY LOVER   ⟅ DO IT WHILE THE DINNER'S COOKING
♋ A LITTLE CONTORTION   ♀ NO EQUIPMENT REQUIRED

The attic is part of the house but at the same time not part of the house. It sits on top, detached. Maybe it's the place for things that just wouldn't be quite right anywhere else.

The *Kama Sutra* recommends having one room in the house, a pretty environment designed only for love. On the table are the herbs for the protection of the gods as well as drawing materials, illustrated books, and garlands of flowers or rose petals. A circular rug with bolster cushions for lounging. Plants and other natural decoration. A secret room for fantasies and role play. Why not convert your attic?

Put a closet in the corner. In it hang different outfits and costumes, each there for a different role play. Open the doors and who knows what you might find. And up in the attic, it's safe to explore these fantasies. It's like Narnia for adults.

In the center of the room, standing like an erect totem, is the lapdancing pole. Something to play with, to dance around. On the walls are hooks and handcuffs, symbols of the games that you and your partner might play.

The attic is your secret fantasy playground. Anything goes. Anything is possible.

～ *Telephone* SEX ～

You're upstairs in the attic, sorting a few things out, searching around in all the nooks and crannies, moving boxes around, trying to get to whatever it was you were up there to get. You feel your cell phone in your back pocket and . . . There's an idea. You speed dial "home." You hear the phone ring downstairs. You know she'll pick it up. And she does.

She doesn't recognize your voice immediately.

"What are you wearing?" you say.

"Wha . . .?" But she takes a breath and remembers the last time she played this game. She tells you in a slow breathy voice what you want to hear.

"Take it off." Your voice is authoritative.

She settles onto the sofa, phone in hand as you demand more information. You're in your den, and nobody knows how you'll make use of what she tells you. The ancient tantrics believed that it takes two happy souls to make a partnership, and that means learning how to pleasure yourself first. Let the winds of Heaven dance between you . . .

♥ EASY LOVER   ✘ NEEDS A SLOW HAND
♨ NO CONTORTION REQUIRED   ♈ NO EQUIPMENT REQUIRED

You've always fantasized about being surrounded by naked women, all ready to service you, all ready to be serviced by you.

You're in the attic and you call downstairs for your partner. She comes upstairs to find you lying on the mattress, phone book in hand, leafing through the escort agencies. She is shocked but as you motion for her to come over, you tell her your fantasy. She's intrigued, and not entirely convinced, but you pull her down and start to peel her clothes off telling her how she would be the star of the show in your own secret attic hideaway—a place where anything is allowed.

She begins to relent a little as you start playing with her body, moving your hands over her, kissing and caressing her, telling her to imagine how it would feel if it were another woman's hand that she felt right now. She asks you whether you would mind. You tell her your time will come. Everyone's time will come.

In the scriptures, group sex is called *Samghataka Rata*. "Two women lie on the same bed and the man makes use of both of them. While he is mounting one, the other, excited, kisses him and after pleasuring one, he brings the other to orgasm."

♡ YOU'LL GET THE HANG OF IT   ✗ NEEDS A SLOW HAND
⚘ NO CONTORTION REQUIRED   ⚑ NO EQUIPMENT REQUIRED

⌢ *Taking It in* HER STRIDE ⌢

Everyone knows about touch, sight, smell, hearing and taste: the five senses. All need to be stimulated in the great game of love. You cannot reach nirvana without stroking each of these. But the wise men and women of the *Kama Sutra* days knew that it wasn't only the senses that needed to be aroused: you also needed to awaken "the six great nerves" (*see pages 108–109*). Touch these and you'll not only turn on the light, you'll provoke violent desire.

Take your time to find your way around them; you won't be disturbed in your secret sacred space; learn them well and you'll be keeping her happy for life. But first, you need to explore. This is as much about contemplating what you've got to enjoy for the rest of your life as satisfying your more immediate needs.

Take your time and, if she is very flexible, help her into *Traivikrama* ("The Stride"). This is a challenging pose, but slow and graceful in its movements. Standing beside your lover, brace yourself with your right leg slightly bent and your right foot just inside her right foot. She bends at the waist and supports her weight on her hands. Place your right hand under her right thigh and lift her leg high

until she can lean her shin against your chest, with her foot pointing over your shoulder. You are in control, but you can barely move.

You are calm and centered, focused on each other and on maintaining balance. Breathe deeply and fill each other with your sexual energy. Vatsayana explains it thus: "She stands on palms and feet; you stand behind her and lift one of her feet to your shoulder."

When you feel ready, pause, and repeat with her left leg raised.

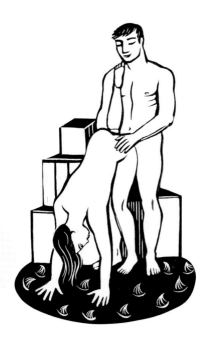

There are six great nerves which, when excited, will produce in a woman the unbearable urge for intercourse. *Sati* is the left part of the vulva and *asati* the right. *Subhaga* and *durbhaga* are to the right and left respectively, a little way in from the entrance to the vagina. And *putri* and *duhitrini* are at the neck of the womb. All of these nerves end in the clitoris.

There are plenty of ways of exciting these nerves. Hugging and caressing both the armpits excite the *sati* and *asati*, according to the *Kama Sutra*. Kissing her face will ignite the *putri*. Think about the heat in the groin that grows with a passionate kiss; Vatsayana says that's the way to ignite the *subhaga*. There's a direct path to the *durbhaga* through caressing the waist. Be careful when you touch her buttocks; according to the ancients, agitation in the *duhitrini* leads to immediate orgasm.

Embracing and touching your partner with these nerves in mind will make her knees weak. Combining the techniques you've learned for scratching and biting (even if this just means running your nails slowly over her body) will be sure to drive her wild with desire.

♡ YOU'LL GET THE HANG OF IT   ✗ DO IT WHILE THE DINNER'S COOKING
    ❧ A LITTLE CONTORTION   ♈ NO EQUIPMENT REQUIRED

When her urges become unbearable, move on to *dhenuka*, an ancient position that calls on your primal instincts and reaches the parts other positions just can't reach. (Next time she accuses you of being bullish, prepare to mount.) "She bends well forward and grips the bedstead, her buttocks raised high; cup your hands to serpents' hoods and squeeze her jar-shaped breasts together: this is '*Dhenuka*,'" wrote Vatsayana. In the attic, she could use that old end-table in place of the bedstead. Just don't tell her that this position translates as "The Cow."

The attic is the best place in the house to be if you want to shut everyone else out. There's no TV, no telephone, no contact with the outside world. They can't get you here. This is the time to meditate into each other, to melt into each other's mind and body.

Turn off the lights. There are a couple of candles on the floor giving off a flickering warm light. Sit facing each other, naked, and look into each other's eyes. Sit in the Lotus (*Padmāsana*) position. Spreading the thighs, he places his right foot on his left thigh and his left foot on his right thigh. You do the same. As you edge closer to each other you see nothing but your partner's eyes. You hear nothing but his breath. Your hands are on your knees, his hands on his. Gradually your gaze blurs and blends, gradually you melt into each other. Do not touch. You feel a stirring in your loins. His lingam swells. Your nipples harden and tingle. Do not touch. The sound of the breath increases and becomes more rapid. Still do not touch.

Vatsayana knew that, in this way, two people could bring each other to orgasm simply by the power of their presence.

♡ YOU'LL GET THE HANG OF IT   ✗ NEEDS A SLOW HAND
♣ A LITTLE CONTORTION   ♀ NO EQUIPMENT REQUIRED

"Love in The Garden" (*Anga Samprayoga*): "Love is easy in the garden, stimulated by beautiful ornaments. It takes place within nature, beneath the arbors, to the sound of the lute." It sounds poetic—and it is. The garden is the perfect place for love and sex. It is where nature expands, where growth occurs. It's the ultimate earthy environment, the place where fertility and life blossom.

For experimental lovers, the garden offers something new for all the senses. From the smell of the outdoors to the raw touch of the grass, it's all there. Ever thought of smearing each other with mud? It's a whole lot sexier than chocolate sauce bought from the local sex shop.

The other thing about the garden is that you're exposed to the elements. In the heat of the summer, does it matter how many homes overlook the garden? You might not be the only ones being turned on.

When it's cold, take a blanket out into the hammock and wrap up warm. Swaying under a wintry sky, studded with stars, feel the warmth of each other and take turns imagining what the evening will bring.

The WORLD *Is*
~ BRIGHT AND NEW ~

It's a beautiful spring day. The sun's shining, and the sky is a beautiful Arctic blue. The trees are starting to wake up and there's a crisp feel in the air. You haven't been in the garden for months but now is the time to sort a few things out.

Take her hand and walk out of the back door, whistling and singing. Kick a few leaves out of the way, clearing the debris. You see that old kissing chair you bought last summer, one of those Victorian pieces with two chairs joined at the hip and facing in opposite directions.

You look around to see who's watching. There is the old lady next door, but she's watering her plants and hasn't noticed you. The people opposite can see into your garden, but they're not looking now. Seated next to each other, you kiss and nibble the thighs, chest, and armpit of your lover in what Vatsayana called *Sama*. Now you seize her breasts, cheeks, buttocks, navel and knead them, your thighs interlaced and squeezing each other urgently, in *Pidita*. *Aschita* is tickling and kissing lightly below the breast and the armpits, while *Mridu* is lightly touching the neck, breasts, buttocks, and back. Kissing in the old style, you awaken her body as the sun awakens the garden you sit in. You strike a spark to ignite the flame of a new season of sexual growth.

⌒ SWINGING LOVERS ⌒

The garden is a place for swingers—but this is nothing to do with cheesy parties or group nibbles. The greatest piece of garden furniture is the hammock. It's almost like it was designed for love.

Lie in a hammock with your partner. Consider the way you roll into each other. There's no escape. You're all rolled up and it's the perfect place to explore each other while staying in one place.

Vatsayana says that it is not possible to count all the parts of the body where men place their lips. "A sexual relationship without preliminaries is incomplete. Desire, affection, love, create a lasting state of mind, through which the boy and girl, stimulated by caresses, abandon themselves wholeheartedly to the act of love."

Try lying lengthways in the hammock. Then try crossways. The rhythm is completely different. The former is rolling and grooving, the latter is swaying and swinging. By the time you've rolled against each other, feeling each other's bodies but not able to move, you'll be ready for what Vatsayana called "going indoors where it's warmer and getting down to the bone."

♡ YOU'LL GET THE HANG OF IT   ✗ DO IT WHILE THE GRASS IS GROWING
   🦎 A LITTLE CONTORTION   ⍾ NO EQUIPMENT REQUIRED

TURNING *Over A*
~ NEW LEAF ~

You're busying yourselves in the garden, getting things in order. The heat of the summer has been replaced by the fading light of the fall, and it's that time of year when the squirrels are collecting their nuts and preparing for withdrawal.

There are leaves everywhere and it's slippery underfoot from all the mulch. In front of you lies a huge mound of leaves, neatly swept and ready to be picked up. You playfully push him over and he falls into the pile of leaves. You fall next to him—it's easy, you won't hurt yourselves—and roll on top of him.

You're both a bit sweaty and hot from the physical work you've been doing and you roll in the mound of leaves to cool off. The mulch of the leaves combined with his sweat and heat . . . You become a slippery, sliding wood nymph. Your clothes are wet as you roll around together, but there's something primal in all this, the feeling of nature on your skin. You start to kiss. Who will be first to seize the other's lips? From your lips, he tunnels into your soaking t-shirt, pulling at your breasts. He sinks into your nipples.

"Kissing with the teeth is an art that must be practiced gently and is particularly efficacious when the tips of the breasts and buttocks are nibbled," said Vatsayana who obviously liked a bit of gardening. "Consider," he wrote, "she climbs upon you, the flowers dropping from her tousled hair, her giggles turning to gasps."

Nooks and crannies are "the right here, right now" areas of your home, the places where you drop your trousers and fling your shirt on the way to somewhere else. They're the unseen corners where the dirt collects; the less than acceptable parts of your home that you keep out of sight, that you sweep under the carpet. But you know what another old philosopher had to say about the whole being the sum of the parts, and your darker thoughts and desires need a place to hang their coats too.

Nooks and crannies are useful for us because they are cramped and tight. It's claustrophobic and dark. You can often feel but not move. It's almost like you're caged.

Quickies don't always have to leave you with your trousers down. Consider your furtive fumbles and secret scratches investment for later. A look, a whisper, even a firm hand reaching into an aching groin is enough to set the scene for what's to come.

Vatsayana reminds us that the art of foreplay is about exciting the imagination as much as pressing the right buttons, and once you've used your shoe cupboard to put away more than your Jimmy Choos, you'll realize that there's really no place quite like home.

⌒ *Where's* YOUR TOOL? ⌒

T he tool cupboard is the place where men like to neatly lay their prized possessions. Ordered and precise, the power drills and screwdrivers lie patiently waiting for the weekend, their battery packs quietly restoring.

This is where he becomes anal, where a false move, a hammer replaced wrongly, can cause him to erupt. The chaos of the outside world is calmed by his meticulously ordered shelves and even the most imaginatively seductive of women could not be forgiven for disturbing the calm of the tool cupboard.

Vatsayana would never have encouraged domestic violence, but a quarrel, he thought, was fair play. Go on, I dare you: spill the nails, mix up the drill bits, and let him find your mess. He'll shout and rant and get steamed up, which is what you want. Take it carefully; you don't want him to get too angry, but a little bit of scratching is at the heart of the *Kama Sutra*, an art in which passions are encouraged to run high.

"Driving the [finger]nails into the ears, the thighs, beneath the shoulder blades or into the brow will arouse desire," wrote Vatsayana.

Press hard enough to leave marks, but do not break the skin. You can't make him any angrier right now, so use that energy for your own selfish ends. See that screwdriver you deliberately put in the wrong place? Go on, try another one, and watch his temperature rise.

Beats putting up another shelf in the bathroom.

⁓ *Dirty* LAUNDRY ⁓

The laundry room might suggest fresh sheets and ironed shirts, but there's no reason why you can't get down and dirty even in here.

Invite your partner in and undress her. Lie her down on the washing machine and lift her legs. This is referred to as *Bhagnaka* in the *Kama Sutra*, where both thighs are raised into the air, exposing her to your element. It's something like folding a clean shirt.

"As her hips begin to churn," wrote the guru, "her head, flung back, bobs ever faster; she scratches, pummels you with small fists, fastens her teeth in your neck, doing unto you what you've often done unto her." If she scratches a lot, practice your knife stroke (*Achchuritaka*): "Slide all five nails to the chosen spot. The thumbnail can be used instead of all the nails together, if it has sufficient effect. Grating may have the same effect as a scratch, even if no cut has been made. A girl should be able to show her scratch marks on her chin and her bottom, even if she does not expose any other nail marks."

As she opens herself to you, flick the switch and turn the washing machine onto full spin. As it rocks and sways, heating her from below, so she will rock and sway, while you take her to the end of the cycle.

♡ YOU'LL GET THE HANG OF IT   ☒ DO IT WHILE THE DINNER'S COOKING
   A LITTLE CONTORTION   NO EQUIPMENT REQUIRED

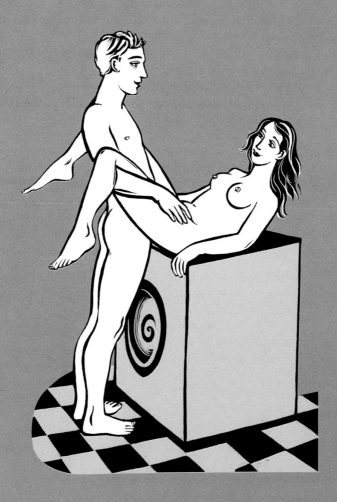

The Best Sex You'll Ever Have, Richard Emerson (Carlton, 2002)

Come Play With Me: Games and Toys for Creative Lovers, Joan Elizabeth Lloyd (Warner Books, 1994)

The Couples Guide to Erotic Games: Bringing Intimacy and Passion Back into Sex and Relationships, Gerald Schoenewolf (Citadel Press, 1998)

The Guide to Getting It On! (The Universe's Coolest and Most Informative Book About Sex) Paul Joaniddes (Goofy Foot Press, 2000)

How To Give Her Absolute Pleasure: Totally Explicit Techniques Every Woman Wants Her Man To Know, Lou Paget (Bantam Doubleday Dell Publishing, 2000)

The Multi-Orgasmic Couple: Sexual Secrets Every Couple Should Know, Mantak Chia and Douglas Abrams (HarperSanFrancisco, 2002)

The New Good Vibrations Guide to Sex, Anne Semans and Cathy Winks (Cleis Press, 1997)

Pucker Up: A Hands-On Guide to Ecstatic Sex, Tristan Taormino (Regan Books, 2001)

Tantra and The Tao, Secrets of Sexual Ectasy, Gilly Smith (Robinson, 1995)

~ *Useful* WEBSITES ~

www.kamasutra-sex.org
Introduction to the *Kama Sutra*—text, explanations of positions, and pictures

www.kamasutra-sexpositions.com
History and illustrations of the positions in the *Kama Sutra*

users.forthnet.gr/ath/nektar/kma/main.htm
kamasutra.openfun.org
Animated guides to the positions of the *Kama Sutra*

www.tantra.com
Online resource for Tantra, Tantric sex and the *Kama Sutra*

www.artofloving.com
Online resource for love and relationships, including a guide to *Kama Sutra* positions and other ideas to enhance your sex life

www.bettydodson.com
A site devoted to masturbation, erotic sex education, and promoting sexual diversity

www.siecus.org
Sexuality and Information Education Council of the U.S.

~ INDEX ~